27 SCRIPTURE SONGS FOR YOUNG VOICES

CAN YOU IMAGINE?

Arranged by Joseph Linn

Piano transcriptions by
Lyndell Leatherman and Joseph Linn

Lillenas Publishing Co.
KANSAS CITY, MO. 64141

CONTENTS

Rock on Rock

(Matt. 7:24-27)

JANETTE SMART

TERRY CAMSEY
Arr. by Joseph Linn

21
G9 G9 C7 9♭ F B♭7 F N.C.
self, 1. "Self, this-'ll do." So he dug foun-
2. "The best will do."
25
C7sus/G C7 F F M9 Dm
da - tions deep down And he built his house and set-tled down, Till one
3
29
G9 2nd time to Coda G7 C7 G7/D C Part 1 B♭ Am C7/G
night when the rain came pour - ing, pour-ing down. Then the
33
F F7 9♯ Part II B♭7
house it shook in the wild, wild wind, And the rain just came a -

37
All
pour-ing in.___ Then the house it start-ed to cave, yes, cave___ in.
41
'Cause it was built on sand,__ sand, sand. Yes, it was shift-ing sand,___ sand, sand.
Optional harmony parts
sand, sand
sand, sand
(walking bass)
45
1
And the house fell down,__ oh yeah,____ with a might-y roar.____
oh yeah,____ with a might-y roar.____

D.S. al Coda
with a might - y roar.
with a might - y roar.
D.S. al Coda
CODA
Part 1
53
But the house stood firm in the strong, strong wind;
Part 2
Not a sin - gle drop of rain got in,
All
And the
57
fam - 'ly was shel - tered safe, quite safe with - in.

61
Bb9
'Cause it was built on rock, rock, rock. Yes, it was sol - id
Optional harmony parts
rock, rock
F6
65
Bb9
1
rock, rock, rock. There is noth - ing that can knock a house built on rock.
rock, rock
can knock a house built on rock.
F
Bb9/F
F
2
Bb9
F
Gm/F
F°
F6
a house built on rock.
a house built on rock.

Half a Million Reasons Medley

(Ps. 118:24; 136)

Arr. by Joseph Linn

*"Half a Million Reasons" (Flo Price)

Happy 𝅗𝅥 = 120

13
E♭ Cm F7 B♭ B♭/A
things that Je - sus does for me I nev - er could af -
G7 17 Cm7 F7
ford; Wish I had a mil - lion ways to praise the
*"O Give Thanks" (Gary Johnson)
B♭ E♭/B♭ B♭ E♭/F F7 21 B♭
Lord. O give thanks to the
25 F7
Lord for He is good, for He is

29
B♭
good. O give thanks to the
33
F7
Lord; His lov - ing kind - ness it will en -
*"O Give Thanks" (Flo Price)
37
B♭ Cm7 B♭7/D E♭ Cm F7
dure. O give thanks to the Lord for He is
41
B♭ Gm7 Cm6
good, And His lov - ing

F7 Bb Cm7 Bb7/D
kind - ness con - tin - ues for - ev - er. O give
45
Eb Cm F7 Bb Bb/A G7 G/F
thanks to the Lord for He is good. Hal - le -
49
Cm/Eb C7/E F sus F7 Bb Ab/Bb Eb/Bb Bb Eb/F F
lu - jah! Praise ye the Lord!
53
Bb Bo7 Cm7 F7
Sing a lit - tle song to Je - sus, praise Him ev-'ry day. Just start

57
Cm7 F7 B♭ Cm7 C♯o B♭/D B♭ Cm7 B♭7/D
count - ing all the bless - ings that He sends your way. And when you
61
E♭ Eo B♭/F G7
start your day out lone - ly, things are fall - in' out of place,
65
Cm7 Dm Cm/E♭ Cm7 Dm Cm/E♭ Cm7 F6 F7
Just keep in mind a day this fine's a ter - ri - ble thing to
69
B♭ Dm7 G6 G7 C Dm7 C7/E
Part 1 (all sing 1st time)
waste. O there's a

71
F Dm G7 C C/B Am
half a mil - lion rea - sons to be thank-ful ev-'ry day, A
Part 2 (sing on repeat only)
thanks to the Lord for He is good, And His
75
Dm6 G7 C Dm7 C7/E
half a mil - lion rea - sons, and I can't be-gin to say All the
lov - ing - kind - ness con - tin - ues for - ev - er. Oh, give
79
F Dm G7 C C/B A7 G/A A7
things that Je - sus does for me I nev-er could af - ford; Wish I
thanks to the Lord for He is good. Hal - le -

83
Dm G7 C
1
Part 1 Dm7 C7/E
had a mil - lion ways to praise the Lord. Divide into 2 parts Oh, there's a
Part II
lu - jah! Praise ___ ye the Lord! Oh, give
2
88
C Dm7 Am/E Dm/F D/F♯ F/G G F/G G7
Hal - le - lu - jah! Praise ___ ye the
Hal - le - lu - jah! Praise ___ ye the
92
C
Lord! Wish I had a mil - lion ways to praise the Lord!

Nobody Else

LINDA REBUCK

(Gen. 1; 6-8; Ex. 3:6,14; John 3:16)

TOM FETTKE
Arr. by Joseph Linn

22
26
29
33
Fm7/B♭ B♭7 E♭ D7 Gm Gm9/F
small. He filled the land with fire - flies, gi - raffes and aard - varks,
ly. So then the Lord said, "Take them all in - to a great big
C9/E B♭/F G7 C9 C7
too. And then He made a talk - ing thing that looks a lot like
boat." And Plan - et Earth was wa - ter-logged, but No - ah stayed a -
Even eighths
F7sus F7
you!
float!
Oh,
Even eighths
E♭ B♭/D Cm7 F7 B♭
no - bod - y else could do that. No - bod - y else could do that.

37
No one ex-cept the great "I AM"; He
41
must be the God of (clap, clap) A - bra - ham.
2nd time to Coda
45
Shuffle resumes
D.S. al Coda
2. As
CODA
N.C.
ham.
51
Shuffle resumes

55
Part 1
Part 2
3. Well, man-y years had come and gone since
many-y years come and gone since
59
No-ah's float-ing zoo, And sin-ful man was still the same: God
No-ah's float-ing zoo, sin-ful man still the same: God
63
knew what He must do. He sent His Son in-to the world to
knew what He must do. He sent His Son in-to the world to

67
Am Em/G Am6/F♯ C/G A7
die up - on a tree, So ev - 'ry - one who trusts in Him will
die up - on a tree, So ev - 'ry - one who trusts in Him will
70 Even eighths
D9 D7 G sus G7
live e - ter - nal - ly. Oh,
Even eighths
74
F C/E Dm7 G7 C
no - bod-y else could do that. No - bod-y else could do that.

78
F C/E E7/G♯ Am Am7 D7
No one ex-cept the great "I AM"; He
1
C/G G7 C
must be the God of A-bra-ham. Oh,
2
C/G C C/G 90 C C/G
must be the God of, He must be the God of, He must be the God of
C
A-bra-ham.

Shout with Joy

(Ps. 100)

D. W.

DAN WHITTEMORE
Arr. by Joseph Linn

F/C C 14 F C
Try to re - al - ize what this means: The Lord is God,
G7 C C7 18 F
the Lord is God. Try to re - al - ize what this
C G7 1 C Dm7 C7
means: The Lord is God, the Lord is God. Try to
2 C 23 C F Dm7
Come through His o - pen gates sing - ing

27
G F/G G F/G F/C C C
Praise in song of thanks - giv - ing, For He is lov - ing and
F Dm7 G F/G G F/G C
kind; His faith - ful - ness is ev - er - last - ing.
31
Part 1
C F Dm7 G F/G G F/G
Come through His o - pen gates sing - ing Praise in song of thanks -
Part 2 (optional)
Come through His o - pen gates sing - ing Praise in song of thanks -
31

35
F/C C C F Dm7
giv - ing, For He is lov - ing and kind; His
giv - ing, For He is lov - ing and kind; His
35
G F/G G F/G C F/C C
All sing 1st time
faith-ful - ness is ev - er - last - ing. Try to
faith-ful - ness is ev - er - last - ing.
40
F C G7
re - al - ize what this means: The Lord is God, the Lord is God.
made us. We are His peo - ple, the sheep of His pas - ture;
40

44
C F C
Try to re - al - ize what this means: The
Shout with joy— He made us. We are His peo -
G7 C Dm7 C7
Lord is God, the Lord is God. Try to
Opt. div.
- ple, the sheep of His pas - ture; He
49
C C7 F C
Try to re - al - ize what this means: The Lord is God,
shout with joy. re - al - ize what this means: The Lord is God,

G7
C Dm7 C7/E
53
F
the Lord is God. Try to re - al - ize what this
the Lord is God. Try to re - al - ize what this
53
C G7 C F/C C
means: The Lord is God, the Lord is God, The Lord is God,
means: Lord is God, the Lord is God, The Lord is God,
57
F/C C F/C C
the Lord is God, the Lord is God.
the Lord is God, the Lord is God.
57

Can You Imagine?

J. S. | (Gen. 1; Ps. 121; Is. 57:15; John 14:23) | JANETTE SMART
Arr. by Joseph Linn

Bm7 Em A7 21 D G
u - ni - verse, His might - y plan in - clud - ed you and me.
comes in - to your heart and says He'll live there, it's for keeps.
D/F♯ Em D Em F° D/F♯ 25 G A9/G
(Me? . . . Really?)
(Forever? . . . Never go away?)
Well, this ex - per - i - ence is not im - ag - in -
F♯m7 B7 29 Em F♯m Em/G E7/G♯ A7sus
a - tion; It's a fact, oh yes, it's true.
A7 G/A A7 33 D Em
And I just can't keep it to my - self; I'll

A7 D G/D D Em/D D A7 D
pass it on to you. 2. Can you im -
D G/D D Em/D D Em F° D/F♯
you. Well, this ex -
45
G A9/G F♯m7 B7 B7/D♯
per - i - ence is not im - ag - in - a - tion; It's a
49
Em F♯m7 Em/G E7/G♯ A7sus A7
fact, oh yes, it's true. And I

53
D Bm7 Em A7
just can't keep it to my - self; I'll pass it on to
57
D Bm7 Em A7
you. Can't keep it to my - self; I'll pass it— And I
61
D Bm7 Em A7
just can't keep it to my - self; I'll pass it on to
65
D G/D D G/D D A D
you, And you, and you, and you.

What Do You Give a God Who Has Everything?

N. H.

(Prov. 3:5-6; Is. 66:1-2)

NANCY HARRISON
Arr. by Joseph Linn

17
Dm G F
1
Em A
He is the One who flung the shin - ing gal - ax - ies in space.
Give Him your life and let Him guide you,
21
Dm7 D9 D7 G7sus G Am7 G7/B
He is the One who hung the stars in space!
2
Em A
27
Dm7 Dm G6 G7/F
trust Him in all your ways. Give Him your heart; He'll fill it up with
Em A7 Bm7♭5 A7/C♯
31
Dm7 F/G G F/G G7
praise! Give Him your heart; He'll fill it up with

35
G/C C
Ab/Db Db
praise!
Bbm/Eb Ebm
Ab Bbm7 Ab7/C
39
Db Ebm7 Ab6 Ab7
What do you give a God who has
What do you give a God who has
Ab/Db Db
43
Db Ebm7 Ab Gb/Ab
ev - 'ry-thing?
ev - 'ry-thing?
What do you give a God who has it
What do you give the Mak - er of the
Fm Bb7 Cm7 5b Bb7/D
47
Ebm Ab Gb/Ab
all?
earth?
He is the One who flung the shin - ing
Give Him your life and let Him guide you,

1
Fm Bb 51 Ebm7 Eb9 Eb7
gal - ax - ies in space. He is the One who hung the stars in
Ab7sus Ab Bbm7 Ab7/C
space!
2 Fm Bb
trust Him in all your ways.
57 Ebm7 Ebm Ab6 Ab7/Gb Fm Bb7 Cm7 5b Bb7/D
Give Him your heart; He'll fill it up with praise!
61 Ebm7 Gb/Ab Ab Gb/Ab Ab Ab/Db Db Ab/Db Db
Give Him your heart; He'll fill it up with praise!

Jaws

(Daniel 6)

JANETTE SMART

TERRY CAMSEY
Arr. by Joseph Linn

13
got no fear? No pray'rs for thir - ty days, my de - cree; To the
more than a week. Pangs of hun-ger are mak - in' them roar; They're
13
3
lions you'll go, to the lions you'll see some
lick - in' their chops and ask - in' for more in their
17
Cm
ALL
mf
Jaws, jaws,
Cm/Bb
17
(right hand both times)
Stop finger snaps
Fm6/Ab
G7
Cm
Fm6/Ab
G9#/7
21
Cm
Eb
li - on's jaws— Roar - in', crunch-in' li - ons' jaws— Sharp and munch - in',

F
A♭/G♭
Cm/G
G7
Cm6
1
KING DARIUS
hun - gry, snap - pin', crack - in' li - ons' jaws.
2. Yes,
2
28
tacet
mf
30
C♯m
C♯m/B
F♯m
G♯7
C♯m
DANIEL
NARRATOR
DANIEL
3. "Go a - head," said Dan - iel then.
"You can throw me
NARRATOR
4. In they threw him— in - to the den,
And quick - ly shut the
30

34
A6 G♯ C♯m E F♯ A/G
in that den. Lit-tle old lions don't scare me none; my God will
door a-gain. The poor old king could-n't sleep that night, Im-
3
38
C♯m/G♯ N.C. C♯m C♯m/B
ALL
f
keep me safe. I won't run from those Jaws, jaws,
ag-in-ing Dan-iel gulped down in one bite by those
42
F♯m6/A G♯7 C♯m F♯m6/A C♯m E
li-on's jaws— Roar-in', crunch-in', li-ons' jaws— Sharp and munch-in',

F♯ A/G C♯m/G♯ G♯7 C♯m
1st time: repeat
2nd time: go on
hun - gry, snap - pin', crack - in', li - ons' jaws."
47
Dm
49
Dm
NARRATOR
Gm6 A 9♯ 7
5. Ear - ly next morn - in', up with the sun,
mf
½ time feel
Dm Gm6/B♭ A 13♭ 9♭
53
Dm Dm/F
KING DARIUS
Down to the li - ons' den they came. The King says, "Dan - iel,
G B♭/A♭
NARRATOR
N.C.
DANIEL CHOIR
you in there?" And jumps with fright when Dan - iel says, "Yeah!" No

57
Dm
Dm/C
Gm/B♭
A7
Dm
jaws, jaws, li - ons' jaws—
Roar - in', crunch - in',
Gm6/B♭
A9♯/7
61
Dm
Dm/F
G
B♭/A♭
li - ons' jaws—
Sharp and munch - in', hun - gry, snap - pin',
Dm/A
A7
Dm
65
DANIEL (Stronger)
A9♭/7
crack - in', li - ons' jaws.
My God is strong-er than you, oh King;
(finger snaps)
sim.
3
A13♭/9♭
69
Dm
Dm/F
His pro - tec - tion means some-thing.
I don't have a scratch, not e -

KING DARIUS
Gm
B♭/A♭
N.C.
"I'm
- ven a bite ___ 'Cause God sent an an-gel to shut up those, those, those, those . . ."
73
(Sadly)
NARRATOR
A9♭/7
KING DARIUS
sor - ry, Dan - iel," said the King. ___ "My a - pol - o - gies ___
A13♭/9♭
77
Dm
Dm/F
G
B♭/A♭
___ I bring. ___ You were right ___ and I was wrong; ___
N.C.
81
Dm
Dm/C
Sure - ly your God is strong - er than ___ those . . ." Jaws, jaws,

Gm6/B♭ A7 Dm Gm/B♭ A9♯7
li - ons' jaws— Roar - in', crunch - in', li - ons' jaws—
85
Dm Dm/F G B♭/A♭ 1 Dm/A A7 Dm
Sharp and munch-in', hun - gry, snap - pin', crack - in', li - ons' jaws.
2 Dm/A A7
LION 1 LION 2 ALL LIONS
crack - in', li - ons' Pass the ketch-up, pass the mus - tard; For des-sert we got some cus-tard.
NARRATOR
(Breathy)
ALL
Dm6
Don't be sil - ly, don't be has - ty 'Cause the li - ons think you're tas-ty. Jaws!

He's the Children's Savior

B. L.

(Ps. 121:4-8; Mark 10:13-16)

BONNIE LOW
Arr. by Joseph Linn

13
F C7/E Dm
name. He's the chil - dren's Sav - ior, He's the chil - dren's
name.
sim.
15
F/C B♭ C7 F C7
Friend; A ver - y spe - cial per - son and His love will nev - er end. He's the
17
F C7/E Dm Am/C B♭ Gm
chil - dren's Sav - ior, He's the chil - dren's Friend. He's the Lord, and
C 1 F 2 F Part 1
Je - sus is His name. (Solo) 2. When name. He's the

22
F C7/E Dm F/C B♭ C7
chil - dren's Sav - ior, He's the chil - dren's Friend; A ver - y spe-cial per - son and His
Part 2 (optional)
He's the Sav - ior, the chil - dren's Friend; A ver - y spe-cial per - son and His
26
F C F C7/E Dm Am/C B♭
love will nev - er end. He's the chil - dren's Sav - ior, He's the chil - dren's Friend. He's the Lord, and
love will nev - er end. He's the Sav - ior, the chil - dren's Friend. He's the Lord, and
30
C F B♭ Gm C F
Je - sus is His name. He's the Lord, and Je - sus is His name.
Je - sus is His name. He's the Lord, and Je - sus is His name.

By Faith

D. W.

(Gen. 1:26-27; 2:7; Rom. 1:20; Heb. 11:3, 6)

DAN WHITTEMORE
Arr. by Joseph Linn

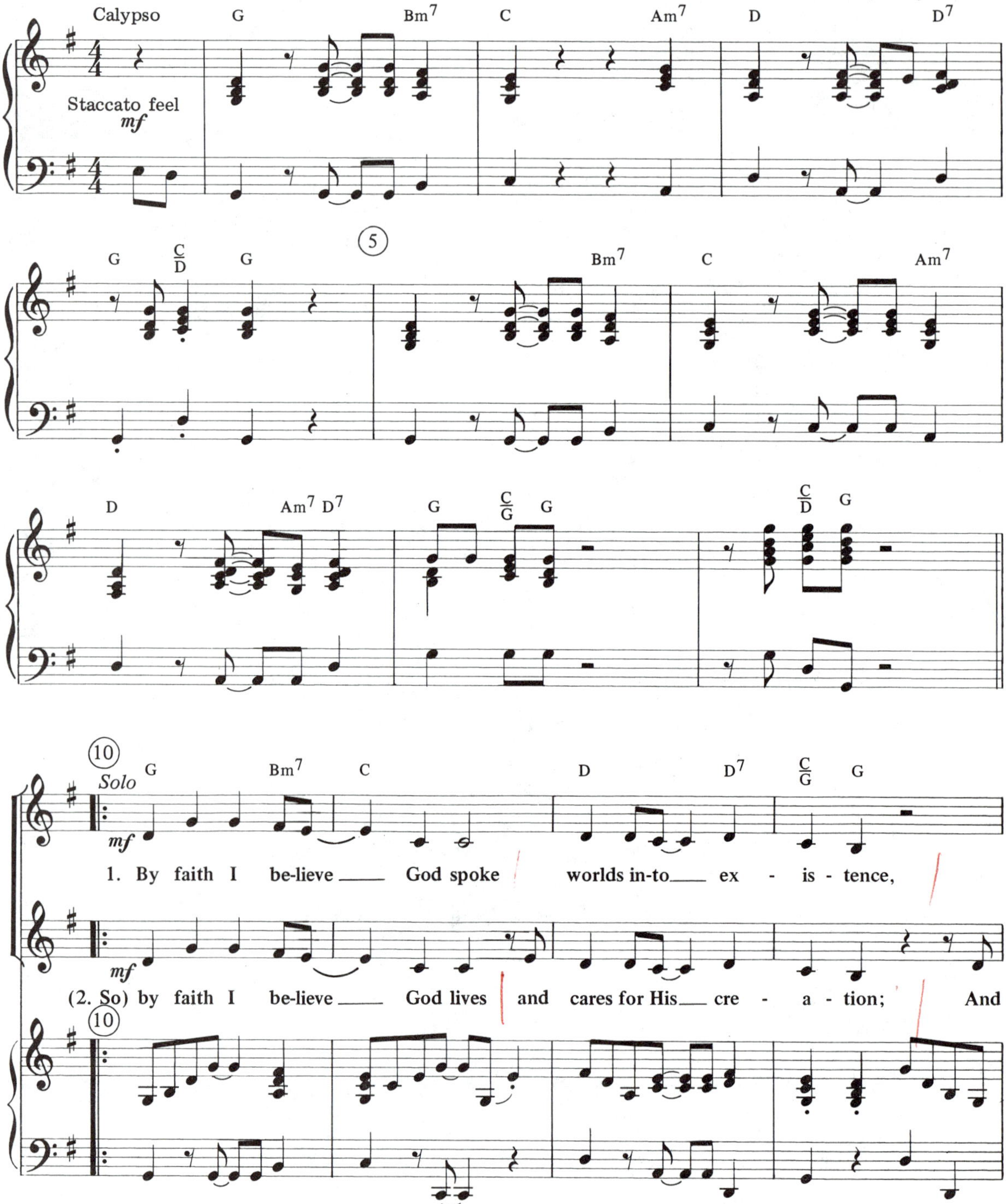

14
G Bm7 C Am7 D D7 G C/D G
So that all I see was made of things I can - not see.
though I of - ten fail Him, He will nev-er turn___ a - way.
14
18
Bm7 C D D7 C/G G
By faith I be-lieve___ God formed the first man in His im - age,
By faith I en - trust in Him this life that He has giv - en; And
18
22
G Bm7 C Am D D7 G C/G G
Breathed in him the breath of life the same He breathed in me.
just as saints of old, by faith His Word I will___ o - bey.
22

Convincingly
All
27
I am not de-scend - ed of mon-keys, Though you may be fooled at first
31
glance. I'm the work of God, my Cre - a - tor; I am not a prod-
35
- uct of chance. I did not e-volve from a tad - pole Who got
39
lost and wan - dered a - shore; But by God's hand, His

G D7 G 1 C D
will, and plan I am and noth - ing more.
G D D7 G Solo
2. So
2 C D G D D7 G C/D G Solo
3. Now
51
G Bm7 C D D7
if per-chance you're still not sure of what I've just been

55
59
63
say - in', Please con - sid - er, if you will, the world and
all ___ you see. God said He re - veals him - self to
all through His cre - a - tion. O - pen up your heart and
by faith sing this song ___ with me: I am
All

68
C G D7 G
Part 1 (all 1st time)
mf
not de-scend - ed of mon - keys, Though you may be fooled at first glance. I'm the
Part 2 (on repeat only)
f
out faith it's im - pos - si - ble to please God. With-
72
C G D7 G
work of God, my Cre - a - tor; I am not a prod - uct of chance.
out faith it's im - pos - si - ble to please God.
76
C G D7
I did not e-volve from a tad - pole Who got lost and wan - dered a -
With - out faith it's im - pos - si - ble to please

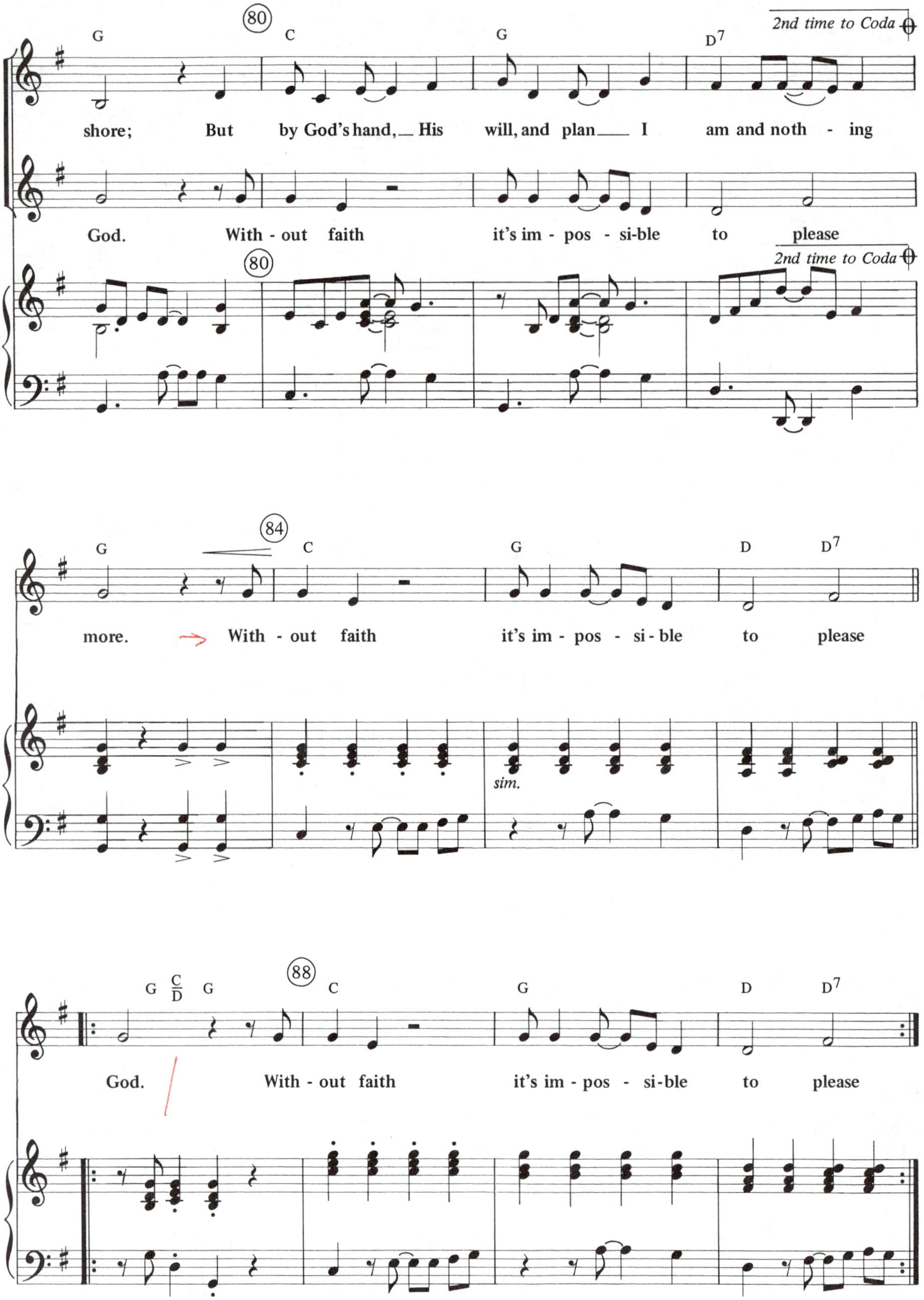
80
2nd time to Coda
G C G D7
shore; But by God's hand, His will, and plan I am and noth - ing
God. With - out faith it's im - pos - si-ble to please
84
G C G D D7
more. With - out faith it's im - pos - si - ble to please
sim.
88
G C/D G C G D D7
God. With - out faith it's im - pos - si-ble to please

D.S. al Coda
CODA
93
(Strong to the end)
mf
God. I am more. With - out faith it's im - pos-
Part 2 (opt.)
f
With- God With - out faith it's im - pos-
- si - ble to please God. With - out faith
97
it's im - pos - si - ble to please God.

Listen to the Story

(Matt. 2:1-11; Luke 2:1-20; John 20:31)

D. E. W.

DAVID E. WILLIAMS
Arr. by Joseph Linn

F♯m9 B7 E 17 E
Sto - ry of the Fa - ther's Son! Born as a ba - by in the
You can come just as ___ you are.
A6 B7 A/E E B A/B 21 E
mid - night, Bring-ing us e - ter - nal day; ___ Came like the
A6 B7 E 1
dawn-ing of the sun - light, Came to take our sins a - way. ___
2 26 F Gm7 C7 Gm7 C

F C7 F
30
F Dm7 B♭ C Gm7
3. An - gels told the sto-ry to a dy - ing world; Lis - ten as we
C7 F
34
F Dm B♭ C
sing it to you. Like the shep-herds looking for the liv - ing Lord,
Gm9 C7 F
38
F
Seek and you will find Him, too. Born as a ba - by in the
B♭6 C7 B♭/F F C B♭/C
mid - night, Bring - ing us e - ter - nal day;

42
F
Bb6
C7
Bb/C
C7
F
Came like the dawn-ing of the sun - light,
Came to take our sins a - way.
1
2
Gm
C
48
mp
Gm
Came to take our
mp
C
F
Gm
Bb/C
C7
sins a - way.
Came to take our sins a -
52
F
way.

Wisemen Still Adore Him

(Matt. 2:1-11; Luke 2:1-20)

D. G.

DWAYNE GOOD
Arr. by Joseph Linn

(Part 2)
(All)
18
23
27
Dm7 G9 Em Am F G9/F
Em Am Am/F# Am/E D9 Gsus G
C/G G C F/C Bb/C F/C
C Bb G7 C F/C
Shep-herds came by night to wor-ship the King;
Wise men from a-far rich of-f'rings did bring
To lay be-fore the feet of the Lord.
Wise men still a-dore Him,
The One born in Beth-le-hem.
Lay your gifts be-fore

B♭/C F/C C/G F/G C
Him; In your heart He'll be born a - gain.
31
F G9/D Em Am F G9/D Em
Come to Beth - le - hem and see Him whose birth the an - gels
Am
35
F G9/F Em Am Am/F♯ Am/E D6 D7
sing; Come a - dore on bend - ed knee Christ, the Lord, the
G sus G N.C.
40
D♭ G♭
new - born King. Wise men

44
Db Cb Absus Ab Db
still a-dore Him, The One in Beth-le-hem. Lay
Gb Db/Ab Gb/Ab Db N.C.
your gifts be-fore Him; In your heart He'll be born a-gain.
48
Part 1
D G D C A7sus
Wise men still a-dore Him, The One born in Beth-le-hem.
Part 2
Wise men still a-dore Him, The One in Beth-le-hem.

52
D G D/A G/A D
Lay your gifts be-fore Him; In your heart He'll be born a-gain.
Lay your gifts be-fore Him; In your heart He'll be born a-gain.
52
56
D G/D C/D G/D D/A A7 D GM9 G6
Lay your gifts be-fore Him; In your heart He'll be born a-gain. In your
Lay your gifts be-fore Him; In your heart He'll be born a-gain. In your
56
60
D/A A D/A A sus A7 D G/D C/D G/A D
heart He'll be born a - gain.
heart He'll be born a - gain.
60

If You Believe

(1 Sam. 17; Dan. 6; Mark 11:24; Acts 16)

M. L.

MOSIE LISTER
Arr. by Joseph Linn

Country 𝅗𝅥 = 120

G
Am
G7/B
21
C7
swung o - pen wide.
If you be - lieve,
G
25
A7
Bm7
you shall re - ceive.
There's not a trou-ble or care the
Cm6
A7/C♯
D
Em
F°
D7/F♯
29
G
good Lord can't re - lieve.
Oh,
He is just the
A7 Enunciate clearly
33
D
same to-day;
All you have to do is just trust and pray and be - lieve,

2nd time to Coda
D7
G
37
G
you must be - lieve.
2. When Dan - iel sat
D
41
D7
with - in the hun - gry li - ons' den, No - bod - y thought
G
45
G
that there was an - y hope for him. But all night long
D
49
D7
the li - ons nev - er took a bite. God took a - way

D.S. al Coda
G
Am
G7/B
their ap - pe - tite.
If you be -
CODA
G
N.C.
Ab
Ebsus
lieve.
3. When Da - vid
57
Ab
Eb
stood be - fore the gi - ant with his sling, Go - li - ath
61
Eb7
Ab
65
Ab
laughed at such a pu - ny lit - tle thing. But Da - vid knew

69
Eb
Eb7
his faith in God would stand the test. He flung the rock; God did the
Ab
Bbm
Ab7/C
73
Db7
rest. If you be - lieve, you shall re -
Ab
77
Bb7
Cm7
C#m6
Bb7/D
ceive. There's not a trou-ble or care the good Lord can't re -
Eb
Fm7
F#o
E7/G
81
Ab
lieve. Oh, He is just the same to-day;

Bb7
85
Eb7
All you have to do is just trust and pray — And be - lieve, you must be -
Ab
89
Eb7
lieve. Be - lieve, you must be -
Ab
93
Eb7
lieve. Be - lieve, you must be -
Ab
lieve.

Clap Your Hands Medley

(Ps. 47)

⑤ *Arr. by Joseph Linn*

Lively 𝅗𝅥 = 132

*"Clap Your Hands" (Jimmy Owens)

G sus G7 C
13
N.C.
mf
voice of praise. Ho - san - na! Ho - san - na! Shout un - to
God with a voice of tri - umph. Praise Him! Praise Him!
17
C G sus G7 C
21
Joyfully
C
Shout un - to God with a voice of praise. Clap your hands,
G sus C G sus C
all ye peo - ple, Shout un - to God with a voice of tri - umph.
Part 2 (opt.)
Clap your hands, all ye peo-ple,

25
C
G sus
C
G sus
C
Clap your hands, all ye peo-ple, Shout un-to God with a voice of praise. Ho-
Shout un-to God with a voice of tri - umph. Clap your hands, all ye peo-ple,
Part 3 (opt.)
Clap your hands, all ye peo-ple, Shout un-to God with a voice of tri - umph.
25

29
C
G sus
C
G sus
C
san - na! Ho - san - na! Shout un-to God with a voice of tri - umph.
Shout un-to God with a voice of praise. Ho - san - na! Ho - san - na!
Clap your hands, all ye peo-ple, Shout un-to God with a voice of praise. Ho -
29

33
C G sus C G sus C
Praise Him! Praise Him! Shout un-to God with a voice of praise.
Shout un-to God with a voice of tri - umph. Praise Him! Praise Him!
san - na! Ho - san - na! Shout un-to God with a voice of tri - umph.
33

37
C G sus C G sus C
Shout un-to God with a voice of praise. Shout un-to God with a voice of praise.
Shout un- to God with a voice of praise. Shout un-to God with a voice of praise.
Praise Him! Praise Him! Shout un-to God with a voice of praise.
37

*"Clap Your Hands" (David Steele)

D A D7 G
D.S. al Coda
CODA
C C/G G7 C
an - swers when we call.
Shout, sing, and praise His name.
59
C/G G C
*"Clap Your Hands" (Gary Johnson)
N.C.
Shout, sing, and praise His name.
Clap your
63
D♭ A♭
hands, shout for joy, Sing to God, ev - 'ry -
D♭ 67 D♭7 G♭
one. Clap your hands, shout for joy, Sing to

Part 1
Part 2
71
Db/Ab Ab7 Db A6 D
God from sun to sun. Clap your hands, shout for
Clap your hands,
A D
joy, Sing to God, ev-'ry - one. Clap your
shout for joy, Sing to God, ev-'ry-one.
75
D7 G D/A A7 D
hands, shout for joy, Sing to God from sun to sun.
Clap your hands, shout for joy, Sing to God from sun to sun.

79
D Unison
A sus D
A sus D
f
Clap your hands, all ye peo-ple, Shout un-to God with a voice of tri - umph.
83
A sus D
A sus D
Part 1
Clap your hands, all ye peo-ple, Shout un-to God with a voice of praise. Ho -
87
A sus D
san - na! Shout un - to God with a
Part 2
Ho - san - na! Shout un - to God with a

91
A sus D A sus D
voice of tri - umph. Praise Him! Shout un - to God with a
voice of tru - umph. Praise Him! Shout un - to God with a
95
A sus A7 D Bm D/A
voice of praise. Shout, sing, and
voice of praise. Shout, sing, and
G/A A7 D G/A A D
praise our God!
praise our God!

Did You Ever Talk to God? Medley

(Ps. 91:15; Mark 11:24; Phil. 4:6-7)

Arr. by Joseph Linn

F Am/E Dm 17 Gm Gm7 C
fear He knows. You can know He'll al - ways hear and He will
G7/C C7 F 21 B♭
an - swer prayer. You can whis-per in a crowd to
C7 F Am Dm
Him; You can cry when you're a - lone to Him. You don't have to pray out
25 Gm Gm7 C B♭/C C7 F
loud to Him; He knows your thoughts. On a lof - ty moun-tain

29
B♭ C C7 F Am
peak, He's there. In a mead-ow by a stream, He's
33
Dm Gm Gm7 C B♭/D C7/E
there. An-y-where on earth you go, He's been there from the
37
F B♭ Gm C7
start. Find the an-swer in His Word; it's true. You'll be
41
F Am/E Dm Gm Gm7
2nd time to Coda
strong be-cause He walks with you. By His faith-ful-ness He'll change you,

C G7 C7 F
too. God an - swers prayer.
45
B♭ Gm7
C7 F Am Dm
49
Gm
C B♭/D C7/E F
D.S. al Coda
You can whis-per in a
CODA
C G7 C7 F
too. God an - swers prayer.
rit.
rit.

57
C
Dm/C
G
F/G
G7
C
Gently ♩ = 100
61
*"When We Talk to Him"
(David Steele)
When we
65
Prayerfully
Am
talk to Him, He will hear us; He will
69
Em
C/E
A7
G sus/D
G
lis - ten to all that we say. For the

73
C Gm9 Gm7 Gb7 5# F M7 F6 Bb9
Lord of all is our clos - est Friend; He is
77
C G F/G C Ab7 Gb/Ab Ab7
Part 1
with __ us as now we pray. __ When we
81
Db Bbm
talk to Him, __ He will hear __ us; __ He will
Part 2
When we talk to Him, __ He will hear __ us; He will
81
l.h. cross over

85
Fm Db/F Bb7 Absus/Eb Ab Ab7/Eb
lis - ten to all that we say. For the
lis - ten to all that we say. For the
85
89
Db Abm9 Abm7 G7 5# GbM7 Gb6 Cb9
Lord of all is our clos - est Friend; He is
Lord of all is our clos - est Friend; He is
89
93
Db/Ab Ab Gb/Ab Db
with us as now we pray. He will
with us as now we pray.
93

97
D♭
B♭m
hear __ us; __ He will lis - ten. __ He is
hear __ us; lis - ten. He is
97
101
D♭
A♭
G♭/A♭
D♭
A♭/D♭
with __ us as now we pray. __
with us as now we pray. __
101
105
G♭/D♭
rit.
G♭m/D♭
D♭
(5)
mp
A - men. __ (nn)
rit.
mp
A - men. __ (nn)
105
mp
rit.

Jesus Is His Name

(Matt. 1:21; Luke 2:1-20; John 1:10-11; Rev. 17:14)

P. W. and D. W.

PAUL and DONNA WILLIAMS
Arr. by Joseph Linn

13
G F♯m Bm E sus E7
mf
Al - le - lu - ia, al - le - lu - ia! Hear the an - gels
mf
A G/A A
17
D D/F♯ G D
sing. King of Kings and Lord___ of Lords,
Em9 A7 D
21
D D/F♯
Je - sus is His name.___ King of Kings and
G D Em9
2nd time to Coda
A7 D
Lord___ of Lords, Je - sus is His name.___

25
D D/F♯ G D B♭ E♭M7 A7 D
mp
2. Sheep are graz - ing on the hill - side; Shep - herds watch their flocks.
mp sim. mf
29
D D/F♯ G D
An - gels sing, "The King is born.
Em9 A7 D
D.S. al Coda
CODA
A♭ B♭ A♭/B♭ B♭
Je - sus is His name."
34
E♭ E♭/G A♭ E♭ Fm7 B♭7 E♭
3. Shep - herds come to see the Child; Je - sus is His name.

38
Eb Eb/G Ab Eb
Lamb of God so meek and mild;
Fm9 Bb7 Eb Ab Eb
Je - sus is His name.
42
Ab
mf - f
Al - le - lu - ia,
Gm Cm F sus F7 Bb B/Bb
al - le - lu - ia! Hear the an - gels sing.
C/Bb C#/Bb D/Bb
47
Eb Eb/G Ab Eb
King of Kings and Lord of Lords,

51
Fm9 Bb7 Eb Bb/F Eb/G Bb Eb Eb/G
Je - sus is His name. King of Kings and
Ab Eb Fm9 Bb7 1 Eb
Lord of Lords, Je - sus is His name.
56
2 Eb Bb/F Eb/G Bb Eb Eb/G Ab Eb
King of Kings and Lord of Lords,
Fm9 Bbsus Bb Eb Bb/Eb Eb Bb Eb Bb Eb Bb Eb Bb Eb Bb Eb Bb Eb
Je - sus is His name.

I Just Want to Be

(Rom. 12:1-2)

A. C. and C. G.

ANDRAE CROUCH and CLARK GASSMAN
Arr. by Joseph Linn

2nd time to Coda
B7 Em A7/E A7♭5/E♭ G/D D7 G C/G G
will is for me, And I'll be what You want me to be. I'll be a
live it for You; I'll do what You want me to do.
13
A B♭ B
work-er, a help-er, a fish-er of men; As faith-ful a ser-vant as
8va
B♭7 A B♭/A♭ 17 G F7 E♭7
there's ev-er been. I'll be a teach-er if You want; I'll be a lead-er if You want 'Cause I
(8va) loco
D C/D D6 D7 G/D D C/D 21 G Am G/B C G/D
love You, Je - sus, praise Your name.

D.S. al Coda
B7 Em A7 A7/E A7/E♭ G/D D7 G C/G G
CODA
G C/G G
26
A A
I will hear You when You call, when - ev - er You speak.
8va
B♭ B B♭7 A B♭/A♭
I will fear You most of all; You're strong and I'm weak. I will
(8va)
30
G F7 E♭7 D C/D D6 D7
trust You ev - 'ry day; I will fol-low You all the way 'Cause I love You, Je - sus,
(8va)
loco

G/D D C/D Am Bm Am/C A7/C♯ D sus
35
G Am G/B C G/D
praise Your name.
I just want to be what You
B7 Em A7 D7
want me to be; I'll be what You want me to be.
39
G Am G/B C G/D B7 Em A7 A7/E A7/E♭ G/D D7 Em
Lord, oh, help me see what Your will is for me, And I'll do what You want me to do.
A7/E A7/E♭ G/D D7 Em7
43
A7/E A7/E♭ G/D D7 G
I'll be what You want me to be.

Sing Alleluia

(Ps. 100)

G. J.

GARY JOHNSON
Arr. by Joseph Linn

18
A Dm A Dm
giv - ing, Come be-fore Him with sing - ing. Bless - ed
Gm Gm6 Gm Dm/A A7 Dm C7
be the God of Is - rael; We are the chil-dren of the King!
22
F B♭ F C7
Come sing al - le - lu - ia, Come sing al - le - lu -
26
2nd time to Coda
F B♭ F C7
ia, Come sing al - le - lu - ia, Come sing al - le -

30
Part 1
lu - ia. Come sing al - le - lu - ia, Come sing
Part 2
Sing al - le - lu - ia, sing al - le - lu - ia, Sing al - le -
34
al - le - lu - ia, Come sing al - le - lu - ia,
lu - ia to the Lord. Sing al - le - lu - ia, sing al - le - lu - ia,
D.S. al Coda
CODA
Come sing al - le - lu - ia. Come sing al - le - lu - ia.
Sing al - le - lu - ia to the Lord. Come sing al - le - lu - ia.
8va

Moses, You're Not Listening

JANETTE SMART (Ex. 3:1-4:17) TERRY CAMSEY
Arr. by Joseph Linn

17
Gm D7 Gm D7 Gm D7
Mo - ses turned and would have run a - way
Mo - ses would - n't see; he fret - ted and he fumed,
God him - self would in His plan pro - vide a way
G sus G
21
C Gm C6 C7 F
Be - cause he felt un - wor - thy and a - fraid.
And made ex - cus - es hour af - ter hour.
To lead His peo - ple to their prom - ised home.
1 Somewhat despairingly
Solo
25
Gm Gm/F C7/E C7 F
Oh, Lord, I am no good. Oh, Lord, I
Am7/E Dm
29
C/G G7 C7
am no good. I can - not speak, I on - ly s - s - s -

33
F C/G F/A F/C B♭ B♭/A Gm C7 F
stut-ter. So that when I have to talk, Yes, when I
Choir
s-s-s - stut-ter.
Am7/E Dm 37 G sus G7 C7 G
have to talk, I put my head down and I m-m-m - mut-ter.
m-m-m-
41
C C7 F C7 F Am7 B♭ D7/A
No one lis - tens; all they do is la-la-la-la-la-la-
mut-ter. No one lis - tens;

Gm D7 45 Gm D7 Gm G7 C7
laugh. You want a man, but I am on - ly ha - ha - ha - ha - ha - ha -
all they do is la - la - laugh. You want a man, but
C C7 49 F C7 F F7 Bb D7 Gm
half. Oh, Lord, will You for - get me; You know they'll nev - er let me
I am on - ly ha - ha - half. You know they'll nev - er let me
53 C sus C C7 F C/G F7/A
be their lead - er. (spoken) Not me!
be their lead - er. Some - one else can do it. And God said,

57 Choir
"Mo - ses, you're not lis - t'ning, You're not
61
lis - t'ning, you're not lis - t'ning. Not in your
65
own strength but by My might.
69
Lis - ten to Me; I will make it al - right." And God said,
N.C.

73
B♭ B♭/A Gm C9
D.C.
"Mo - ses, you're not . . . (spoken) Mo - ses, you're not lis - t'ning."
2
Dm6
Hushed
79
Dm6
mp
Oh, Mo-ses then was in for a sur - prise, For
8va
Eb♭m6
83
Em6 Building
God is might-y pow-er - ful and wise. He turned a rod in - to a snake, then
Building
Fm6 F♯m6 Gm6
D.C.
Solo
turned a snake in - to a rod. He with-ered Mo-ses' hand; then healed it right be-fore his eyes. Wow!

3
F C/G F6/A
88
B♭ B♭/A Gm C9 B♭/F F
And God said, "Mo - ses, now you're lis - t'ning,
D7 9♭
92
Gm11 Gm C7 Gm/F F
Now you're lis - t'ning, now you're lis - t'ning.
C7/G F7/A
96
B♭ B♭/A Gm C9 B♭/F F
Not in your own strength but by My might.
Dm7
100
G9 G9 N.C.
Now you be-lieve; I will make it al - right."

104
C/G F7/A B♭ B♭/A Gm C9 B♭/F F
And God said, "Mo - ses, thanks for lis - t'ning,
108
D9♭7 Gm11 Gm C7 Gm/F F
Thanks for lis - t'ning, thanks for lis - t'ning."
112
C/G F7/A B♭ B/A Gm C9 B♭/F F
And God said, "Mo - ses, thanks for lis - t'ning.
116
D9♭7 Gm sus N.C.
Solo
Mo - ses, you're al - right!"
8va
8va

No Mountain High Enough

C. K.

(Rom. 8:35-39)

CHARLES KIRBY
Arr. by Joseph Linn

2nd time to Coda
No dark - ness black e - nough to keep me from my Lord.
No pow - er strong e - nough to keep me from my
22
mf
There is no moun-tain high e-nough, no riv - er
26
wide e-nough, No o - cean deep e-nough to sep-a-rate me from God.
D.S. al Coda
CODA
N.C.
33
Lord. There is no moun-tain

37
F F♯7 B7 E
high e-nough, no riv - er wide e-nough, No o - cean
C♯m7 Am6/C E/B B7 E F♯m7 E7/G♯
41
A B7
deep e-nough to sep-a-rate me from God. No des - ert
E F♯m7 B7 E E7
45
A E/G♯ B7/F♯
dry e-nough, no jun - gle thick e-nough, No dark-ness
E G♯7/B♯ C♯m7 C♯7 F♯ B N.C.
black e - nough to keep me from my Lord.

51
C9 F F♯ G7
There is no moun-tain high e-nough, no riv - er
C7 55 F Dm7 B♭m6/D♭ F/C C7
wide e-nough, No o - cean deep e-nough to sep - a - rate me from
F C6 Gm/E 59 F Dm B♭m6/D♭ F/C C7
God. No o - cean deep e-nough to sep - a - rate me from
F 63 C7 F Dm B♭m6/D♭ G9/D C7 F
God, To sep - a - rate me from God.
8va

God of Miracles

LINDA REBUCK

TOM FETTKE
Arr. by Joseph Linn

(Ex. 12, 14, 16, 17; 1 Pet. 5:7)

Slow "one" feel 𝅗𝅥. = 48

21
Em
C/E
Am
Am/D
D6
D7
G sus
ev - 'ry need, Who sees through time and space.
25
G
C/E
C
F
He knows our pain and sor - row, And
l.h.
29
D/F#
D
G
33
E/G#
we can come to Him When - ev - er
E
Am
Am/G
37
F
Em
Dm7
f
we have prob - lems, What - ev - er the time or
f

place. Our God is a God of mir - a -
cles, A God of love and grace.
2nd time to Coda
rit.
Slower
He fed the hun - gry peo - ple in the
wild - er - ness With man - na on the

Bb/F Gm/F A sus/E A A7/E
ground when they a - woke. He
59
Dm Dm/C G7/B
made a faith - ful lead - er out of Mo - ses;
Bbm7 Eb9 63 F Dm G9
And e - ven Pha - raoh lis - tened when He
C sus C C7 67 March style F
spoke. He o - pened up the

E♭M7 E♭M9 C/F F C/F F
71
Red Sea for His peo - ple; They walked right
3
E♭M7 E♭M9 A sus/E A7 A7/C♯
through and fled the en - e - my. He
75
Dm Dm/C G/B
gave them wa - ter from a rock when thir - sty.
B♭m7 E♭9 F Dm G9
They had been slaves, but God had made them
3/4

81
Quicker, Tempo I
C C/B♭ A♭M7 Csus/G C
D.S. al Coda
free. Our
CODA
F/G G♯o Am C/G
88
F G/F
love and grace. Our God is a God of
Em C/E Cm/E♭
92
Dm F/G G7
mir - a - cles, A God of love and
C F/C F/G G7 rit. C
grace, love and grace.
rit.

The Sower Parable

(Matt. 13)

D. W. — DAN WHITTEMORE
Arr. by Joseph Linn

Strong 𝅗𝅥 = 76

13
E
Solo 1
E/G♯
Solo 2
All
Some on the road, some in the weeds, But
A
F♯7
17
E
ev - 'ry-where you look you find lit - tle bit - ty seeds. The Word of God is like
B7
B6
B7
E
Lighten up
lit - tle bit - ty seeds, Scat-tered all a - round. 1. Now the
21
E
B
seed that falls in the mid-dle of the road, Well, the birds steal it a - way.
sim.

B
25
B7
The seed that falls in the mid-dle of the road, The
E
29
E
birds steal it a - way. Well, the road com-pares to
E7/G♯
A
F♯7
an - y man's heart Who re - jects the Word from the ver - y start. The
33
E
B7
B6
B7
seed that falls in the mid-dle of the road, Well, the birds steal it a - way.
sim.

E C7 37 F
2. Now what a - bout the seed that falls in the weeds, That
No ped.
C 41 C7
does-n't pro - duce much grain? What a - bout the seed that
F
falls in the weeds, That does-n't pro - duce much grain? You can
45 F B♭
hear the Word but still live in strife If your greed, like the weeds, chokes

49
G7 F C7
out the life. It's just like the seed that falls in the weeds; It
sim.
C6 C7 E♭add9 B♭ B♭/C
53
F
won't pro-duce much grain. The Word of God is like
resume ped.
C7
lit-tle bit-ty seeds, Scat-tered all a-round. The
57
C7 F
Word of God is like lit-tle bit-ty seeds, Scat-tered all a-round.

Solo 1
Some on the road,
Solo 2
some in the weeds,
All
But ev-'ry-where you look you find lit-tle bit-ty seeds. The Word of God — is like lit-tle bit-ty seeds, Scat-tered all a-round. —
Lighten up
3. Now I want the Word to grow in my heart, Like seeds on fer-tile ground.
sim.

73
D♭7
I want the Word to grow in my heart, Like
G♭
77
G♭
seeds on fer-tile ground. Wa-tered by the Spir-it,
G♭/B♭
C♭
A♭7
touched by the sun, And liv-ing like I should un-til the har-vest comes.
81
G♭
D♭7
D♭6
D♭7
I want the Word to grow in my heart, Like seeds on fer-tile ground.
sim.

Gb N.C. Stronger
85
G
The Word of God is like lit-tle bit-ty seeds,
f
D
89
D7
Scat-tered all a-round. The Word of God is like lit-tle bit-ty
G
93
G
Solo 1
seeds, Scat-tered all a-round. Some on the road,
G/B
Solo 2
All
C
A7
some in the weeds, But ev-'ry-where you look you find lit-tle bit-ty seeds. The

97
G D7 D6 D7 F add9
Word of God is like lit-tle bit-ty seeds, Scat-tered all a-round.
C
101
G G/B
Solo 1 Solo 2 All
Some on the road, some in the weeds, But
C A7
105
G
ev-'ry-where you look you find lit-tle bit-ty seeds. The Word of God is like
D7 D6 D7 F add9 C G
lit-tle bit-ty seeds, Scat-tered all a-round.

What Shall We Children Bring?

(Ps. 50:12, 14; Is. 66:1-2; Mic. 6:8)

From *The Book of Praise for Children,* 1881.

JOE E. PARKS

17
of - fer to the King. We have no wealth or
of - fer to the King; And these are gifts that
1
D.S.
learn - ing; What shall we chil - dren bring? 2. We'll
e - ven The
2
poor - est child may bring.
25
slight rit.